Mountain Mover

By Queen Majeeda

TEACH Services, Inc.
PUBLISHING
www.TEACHServices.com • (800) 367-1844

World rights reserved. This book or any portion thereof may not be copied or reproduced in any form or manner whatever, except as provided by law, without the written permission of the publisher, except by a reviewer who may quote brief passages in a review.

The author assumes full responsibility for the accuracy of all facts and quotations as cited in this book. The opinions expressed in this book are the author's personal views and interpretations, and do not necessarily reflect those of the publisher.

This book is provided with the understanding that the publisher is not engaged in giving spiritual, legal, medical, or other professional advice. If authoritative advice is needed, the reader should seek the counsel of a competent professional.

Copyright © 2018 Queen Majeeda

Copyright © 2018 TEACH Services, Inc.

ISBN-13: 978-1-4796-0891-1 (Paperback)

ISBN-13: 978-1-4796-0892-8 (ePub)

Library of Congress Control Number: 2018937820

All scripture quotations, unless otherwise stated, are taken from the
King James Version of the Bible. Public domain.
Scripture quotations marked (NKJV) is taken from the New King James Version®. Copyright © 1982 by Thomas Nelson. Used by permission. All rights reserved.

Image Credits: Cover, denbelitsky; pg. 7, Eugene Kalenkovich; pg. 20, kated; pg. 21, Zigi; pg. 22, RS Photograpy; pg. 28, litts; pg. 45, dk_photo

Table of Contents

Acknowledgements 5
Prologue 7
POEM   "Mountain Mover" 9
CHAPTER ONE   In Dire Straits 11
CHAPTER TWO   God 13
CHAPTER THREE   Deciding to Trust God 15
CHAPTER FOUR   No Deadline With God 17
CHAPTER FIVE   On the Spot Admission 20
CHAPTER SIX   God Dispatches His Angels 22
CHAPTER SEVEN   Right on Time 25
CHAPTER EIGHT   God Intervenes 28
CHAPTER NINE   God Works Through Friends and a Stranger ... 32
CHAPTER TEN   An Immediate Answer to Prayer 36
CHAPTER ELEVEN He Leads Me 40
CHAPTER TWELVE Working for the Lord 45
Postscript 47
Epilogue 49
Bibliography 51

Acknowledgements

God has given me a story to tell, and I am eternally grateful to Him. I praise Him for His salvation and provision, and I thank Him for the many times He has forgiven me when I fail Him. I am thankful to Him for putting me on track when I lose my way and for giving me the opportunity to know Him more, thus giving me the joy of loving Him more. He has sent many people to be a part of my journey. I am blessed to have had the love, support, assistance, and encouragement of friends, relatives, and strangers who were well-wishers. What I have accomplished could not be done without the support of people who cheered me on while on the journey. I am grateful to my praying mom, Beryl Waysome, who assisted me with finances and many other countless means of support throughout my college years and entire life.

To all those who would say, "You have to write a book," each time they witnessed God's intervention in my life, thank you. Many thanks to all those who offered assistance to me while I was pursuing higher education, including Mekana Lorne, my brother Herman Hamilton, father Norman Hamilton, Jacqueline Wright for offering me a place to stay, Fred Roonie, Marlene "Linny" Fowler and her husband William "Beall" Fowler, Rudy Sterling, my cousin Gene Henriques, Juliett Thomas, Heather Smith, Donnette Tracy, Ted and Racquel Bromfield, David and Trudy Lutchmansingh, Pastor Allan Hay for his prayers and encouragement, the members of New Rochelle Seventh-day Adventist Church and Springfield Gardens Seventh-day Adventist Church, my cousin Gloria Ramsay, who would tell me about any babysitting or eldercare jobs she knew of and recommended me for so I could have some money at times, and to Mitch Owen from 3ABN's Prayer Department who asked, "Have you ever thought of writing a book?" The Lord used you to encourage me just when I began thinking the task would be too daunting. To Pastor Joe O'Brien who also prayed with me numerous times when I called 3ABN'S Prayer Line and has offered so much encouragement and many words of wisdom. If I have forgotten to mention anyone here, I certainly have not forgotten the role you took on in aiding me on my journey. I know I could not have done it alone. Thank you!

Prologue

I became a recording artist in my early twenties. At twenty-four I had a record distribution deal with Heartbeat Records and enjoyed writing, performing, and doing poetry-writing workshops in Jamaica and the United States. I remember one day standing in High Times Records, downtown in Kingston, Jamaica.

"You have to get rid of your passport name," Earl "Chinna" Smith said to me as he listened to the songs I had already completed for my debut album, *Conscious*. "You nuh see all a de poets dem have a stage name."

"Don't you see all the poets have a stage name?"

Chinna, as everyone called him, was the lead guitarist for Bob Marley and the Wailers and played on countless other famous reggae artists' albums.

It was true; virtually all the poets in Jamaica assumed a stage name, so I went to the African Caribbean Institute and searched a book of names. When I came across the name *Majeeda* and its meaning, I decided that my stage name would be Queen Majeeda, and this is the name under which I recorded and performed. *Majeeda* is West African for "noble" or "glorious."

Coincidentally, it seemed, just before the release of my album, I became a Christian. I would say I was a closet Christian, as only my friends knew. I had not told anyone in the industry, as I did not know how to let them know that an Afrocentric poet was worshipping Jesus. To be Afrocentric in Jamaica meant rejecting a "white God." I was worshipping the God of creation, a loving Jew who made all nations, but who would want to hear that? The after-effects of slavery had left many who were in touch with their "roots" rejecting the picture of a Caucasian that was often seen on a calendar. I knew that was not a painting of God. I did not worship that image or any image for that matter. Still, I did not know how to tell the music industry folk. I just did not want to start a debate, so I kept quiet about it. My religion is personal, I reasoned.

On one of my trips to New York to do some recording, I decided to pursue higher education. I did it all by faith, as at the time, I was not earning much money from my recordings or performances. It is one of the best decisions I ever made besides accepting the Lord as my personal Savior. I put my plans in God's hands and He has proven to be my Best Friend and Way-Maker.

> *I put my plans in God's hands and He has proven to be my Best Friend and Way-Maker.*

He has worked through many others to send me help when I needed it and has revealed Himself to be faithful to His promise to give us the desires of our hearts. I wrote this book because of His mercy towards me and because of the many miracles He has wrought in my life. He has given me a story to tell. Yes, I was a Christian before I started college in New York, but today I am a mature Christian who knows the power of God personally. Today, I am not afraid to say I am a Christian. I am older and wiser and have grown closer to God.

Mountain Mover
by Queen Majeeda

Mountain Mover,
is there anything too hard for You?

You walked on water,
You raised Jairus' daughter,
turned water into wine,
raised a widow's son to life.
You claimed power over nature,
turned a prostitute into a woman of virtue.
You calmed the storm at sea,
You were triumphant over every disease.
In You the Father is well pleased.
You healed lepers, the blind, the deaf, the dumb, the lame,
You raised Lazarus from the grave.
You fed more than five thousand,
You conquered death through your own resurrection.
Mountain Mover,
Is there anything too hard for You?

You became one of us.
You healed the ear of Malchus,
as they arrested You in Gethsemane.
You were forgiving of your enemies.
Son of man,
You were God on a mission,
casting out demons who claimed to be legion.
You spoke healing to the sick,
healed the lunatic and the paralytic,
healed the woman with the issue of blood.
My Lord and my God!
It was You who parted the Red Sea,
and spoke this world into being.
You formed clay into a living being,
took a rib from his side,
and created his bride.
You gave the Ten Commandments,

manna to Your people in the wilderness,
You were the Cloud by day and the Fire by night,
in you we find everlasting life.
Great Emancipator,
You have made us more than conquerors.
Oh Mountain Mover,
there is nothing too hard for You!

> *Behold, I am the LORD, the God of all flesh:*
> *is there anything too hard for me? – (Jeremiah 32:27)*

CHAPTER ONE
In Dire Straits

> *"Offer unto God thanksgiving; and pay thy vows unto the most High: And call upon me in the day of trouble: I will deliver thee, and thou shalt glorify me" (Ps. 50:14, 15, KJV).*

I sat at the edge of the chair across from the assistant dean as she scrolled down her computer screen to look at my college record. I was literally on edge and my heart sank into great disappointment when she said, "I see that you default on your payment arrangement every semester. The school is no longer going to allow students who default on their loans to register for the new semester."

I anxiously replied, "But as you can see, my debt for every semester is always paid. It was not intentional on my part to default on the payment arrangements."

As she continued perusing my record, my eyes caught a plaque on the wall unit behind her which read, "Dear Lord, help me to remember that nothing will happen today that You and I can't handle."

I cheered up and said to myself, *absolutely right!* Certainly, with a plaque like that in her office, she knows what it is like to totally rely on God. She'll understand. But I was wrong. Instead, I heard her repeat, "The school is no longer going to allow students who default on their loans to register for the new semester."

My heart dropped. I had an outstanding balance, and I needed an extension so I could have more time to pay and register for the new semester.

"The school does not have any money," she continued.

"I am going to pay my balance, I just need an extension until Monday," I pleaded with her, still not knowing where I would get the money to cover the outstanding balance and pay for the new semester. Like every other semester before, I had trusted God to provide, and He always had—through family, friends, or a job. However, at this time I had no job and no other source of money. I literally had only a prayer.

"My Father is going to give me the money again to pay," I told her, referring to the Sustainer of all life, but she did not sense the differentiation, and, I suppose, she did not care.

Her only other reply was that the deadline to register was Friday—a day away—and that I could try talking to the bursar to see if I would be allowed to register. She was not going to give me a chance to pay on Monday.

Any further pleas on my part did not move her. Instead of granting me an extension, the assistant dean sent me back to the bursar's office to see if she could help me.

After I had explained my situation there, the cashier in the bursar's office had sent me to the assistant dean to see if she would grant me an extension. I walked back to the bursar's office feeling discouraged and baffled but still with a spirit of persistence. I told the cashier what the assistant dean said. She spoke with the bursar; the bursar came out and listened to my situation. She seemed compassionate, a tall, slender, middle-aged woman with graying hair. She looked at my records on the computer screen as I stood behind the cashier's glass window. I pointed out to her that although I was always late with paying my outstanding balance, I was always able to pay before the deadline to register for the new semester. She acknowledged that and nodded in agreement. However, she sent me back to the assistant dean and said she is the only one who could allow an extension at this point.

It was almost five o'clock now. I felt like I was being wheeled and tossed to and fro like a yo-yo. I headed back to the assistant dean's office, but when I got there, her office was closed. This was 5:00 p.m. Thursday. I would have to return the following day, which was the deadline to pay any fees in arrears and to register.

I went home and cried and prayed and cried some more. I did not know what to do. The deadline was less than twenty-four hours away. If I did not pay by then, I would not be allowed to register for the new semester. I was an international student, and that meant being in school full time or returning to Jamaica. I was not prepared to go home without completing my bachelor's program.

CHAPTER TWO
God

Our world is made up of people with diverse beliefs and conceptions of who God is. Each individual has an inherent right regarding convictions and expressions of the Divine. That right is one that I acknowledge and respect wholeheartedly. I had embarked on a journey to a foreign land to pursue a degree, which I had not saved for nor was I in any position to take out a loan. I decided to simply trust this Divine Being who has always provided for, protected, and accompanied me throughout life. Should anyone care, I refer to the Maker of all things living as God. There are many different names for this Creator, but God is the universal title every believer in a Supreme Being can identify with. To me, God cannot be narrowed or limited by any definition. God is who and what God will be. God is the great I Am. God is the Self-Existent One. That's the extent to which we can explain God. To define this Creator would reduce Omnipotence, Omnipresence, and Omniscience.

The journey through college allowed me to get closer to God, prove Him over and over and witness first-hand how He cares for each and every one of us. It allowed me to challenge God and watch Him come through for me. I have heard in the past that God loves a challenge because it gives Him the opportunity to show us what a mighty God He is. Often times my prayer for His provision of my tuition would be based on the marvelous things He has done in the past like speaking this world into being (see Gen. 1), parting the Red Sea (see Exod. 14), and providing for the widow who told Elisha the prophet that the creditors had come to take her sons as servants because she could not afford to pay her debt (see 2 Kings 4). These amazing works made me realize that God can do anything if He so desires. He has promised us many times in His word that He would give us the desires of our hearts and provide for all our needs.

> *He has promised us many times in His word that He would give us the desires of our hearts and provide for all our needs.*

I claimed these promises through those prayers I offered, and the examples listed above were just some of God's miraculous works that served as encouragement to me.

"May the Lord answer you in the day of trouble; May the name of the God of Jacob defend you; May He send you help from the sanctuary, And strengthen you out of Zion." – King David, Psalm 20:1–2, NKJV

CHAPTER THREE
Deciding to Trust God

"For I know the thoughts that I think toward you, saith the LORD, thoughts of peace, and not of evil, to give you an expected end" (Jer. 29:11, KJV).

After crying my heart out and begging God to show me what to do because the assistant dean would not grant me an extension, I remembered that even now God could do anything. I needed help immediately so that I could meet the deadline the next day. However, I was still worried and at my wits' end because I could see no way through. That is the human nature to look at our circumstances and then worry instead of looking to the One who can provide the solution. I decided to call Pastor Allan Hay, who was leading the New Haven Seventh-day Adventist congregation in Brooklyn at the time.

When he answered, I said, "Pastor, I am in a jam." He made a joke of my announcement, and I tried to find the humor, but what I had to say was urgent. I was on deadline.

I told him the situation and he said, "I have seen a lot of prayers answered in my office. Come to my office this Sabbath, and we will pray about it after service."

I replied, "I will be there, Pastor, but the deadline is tomorrow."

He said, "Sister, there is no deadline with God."

Right away I knew God would send the money for sure. I just knew it. I believed in the power of prayer. All things are possible with God, and as the human tendency to worry set in because of the deadline, I decided

I had no choice but to trust God to see what He would do. It was often at these times God came through for me; after I have exhausted all possibilities of getting any money, I am then left with nothing to do but to trust Him. The sad thing is I usually worry and worry and worry and God would come through at the last minute. Then I would feel awful about how I made my situation such a burden by wearing myself anxious. I would promise myself and God that I wasn't going to worry anymore whenever I am in dire straits, but that is easier said than done. Until we learn not to make our challenges our focus, we are going to worry. We should focus instead on the Problem-Solver.

Looking back now, I wonder if it was my needless anxiety that caused the seeming delay on God's part. One thing I know for sure is that each time God came through with my tuition; I knew that it could only be God. You will see what I am talking about as I relate these instances.

CHAPTER FOUR
No Deadline With God

*"Behold, I am the LORD, the God of all flesh:
is there anything too hard for me?" (Jer. 32:27, KJV).*

That night I slept peacefully. After being sent back and forth between the bursar's office and the assistant dean's office, going home to cry, then remembering that God can help even at that late hour, I held on to the words, "there is no deadline with God," and worry did not disturb my sleep at all. I was hoping that in the office where lots of prayers were answered, mine would be too. Certainly, I did not have to venture there to have my prayers answered. God hears us from anywhere, but as old-timers used to say, "More prayer, more power." Also, a drowning man clutches to a straw but I knew I wasn't going to drown because I was going to unite in prayer with others to cling to the Rock of Ages. My faith was bolstered.

The next morning I headed to the assistant dean's office to let her know that the bursar had sent me back to her to see if she could allow me an extension until Monday. There was a line outside her door. I joined the line and anxiously waited as the line slowly moved. What would she tell me this morning? Would she send me back to the bursar? Would she still refuse me an extension? The bursar said only the assistant dean could extend the deadline. After about an hour of waiting in line, someone came out from her office and announced that the deadline for payment was extended until Monday.

Hooray, hip-hip-hooray! I wanted to jump for joy. I had no reason to remain in the line. I knew God had started working. Truly, "there's no deadline with God." He will order and rearrange things according to our faith. I asked Him after leaving the line, "Lord, please send me help from east, west, north, and south."

I had the weekend to see how things would unfurl and what exactly would happen in order for me to remain a student here in New York and finish my degree. I was no longer worried. I was excited to see how God would answer.

The following morning I worshipped with the New Haven Seventh-day Adventist congregation, and after the service Pastor Hay asked four elders to join him in his office. There we knelt in a circle and petitioned the Lord to assist me with the money for my tuition.

Friends and family knew of my situation and would call to encourage me and did whatever they could to help. Also, I would take whatever jobs I could find—be it babysitting or eldercare. However, this particular semester would begin after the end of a long summer with several futile attempts to find a job. All I could do was pray that God would send help.

Saturday night, my brother Herman called to say he was going to give me $500. My father also said he had $500 to give me. Another cousin in Massachusetts called to say she was sending me $500, and my friend Mekana in Bermuda called to say she had $500 to give me "because of my faith." My friend did not know my cousin, and no one planned with another and said let us send $500. They just individually decided to send $500 during the same weekend. This was truly an answer to prayer. I was so filled with gratitude for the assistance of my friend and relatives. This was not coincidence. This was divine Providence in action. Not before and not since, have four people who had not planned together, given me money to help me out of any such dire situation.

Now to some people, this may seem like a small amount of money to come up with but picture yourself in a foreign country with zero dollars, no job, and a wonderful opportunity to further your education. You want to make use of the opportunity given you, so you try all moral means to take advantage of it. Finding $3,800 per semester seems expensive because you are on zero but compared to the cost of private universities, it is more than reasonable. Also, furthering your education provides an opportunity to better your current financial situation, so you definitely want to walk through this door of opportunity filled with potential for a brighter future. I was happy for the opportunity and willing to work hard to take advantage of it. Wouldn't you be too? Wouldn't you also want to do all you can to not waste this opportunity?

Monday morning I was headed to York College with $2,000 to pay my outstanding balance and register for the new semester. God had indeed sent help from east, west, north, and south just as I had asked Him. That $2,000 took care of my outstanding balance, now I had to find the deposit for the new semester before the computers drop the classes on the one-week deadline all students had after registering.

CHAPTER FIVE
On the Spot Admission

So how did I end up in New York at the ripe old age of 31 pursuing a college degree? I had come to New York the summer of the year 2000 to do a recording session with a Brooklyn-based producer. After the recordings were completed, I decided to scout out the requirements for pursuing a degree in the United States. It so happened that York College of the City University of New York was having "On the Spot Admission." With "On the Spot Admission," applicants were told immediately upon examination of their school records whether or not they were accepted to the college. I emailed my mom and asked her to send my school records from Jamaica, so she sent them by FedEx. At the end of August, I was accepted at York.

"Classes begin tomorrow," the lady behind the counter of the admissions office smiled and said.

"Oh no, I won't be able to start until January," I replied as I handed her my passport.

"Okay, so you start in January then. Do you want the school to change your visa?"

"Yes," I replied.

"You will need $120 for the student-visa fee and paperwork that I am going to give you to fill out," she said.

That was the start of my adventure. It was the pre-9/11 era when getting a visa to study in the United States was a whole lot easier. One was not required to return to his or her home country to obtain the student's visa if one was already in the States.

CHAPTER FIVE On the Spot Admission

One year later everything changed with the tragedy of the terror attack on the Twin Towers in Manhattan and the Pentagon in Washington, DC. Such unthinkable tragedies changed the entire nation. Everyone I know in New York suffered to some degree from post-traumatic stress disorder—some mild requiring no treatment and others requiring counseling. A friend would sometimes point to a plane flying overhead and say it was flying awfully low.

I also was so shaken by these catastrophes that early one morning just about two weeks later that September, I was scared out of my sleep by a thunderstorm. I woke to the loud clap of thunder and thought we were experiencing a war. *The whole place has become a battleground*, I thought as I cowered in my bed at my friend Jaqui's Brooklyn apartment. Soon, I realized it was thunder. I decided perhaps I should go for counseling. I did one session with the college counselor. I told her I was wondering if I should go back home. When she responded that at least I had somewhere to go back to, I realized how affected everyone was.

> *One year later everything changed with the tragedy of the terror attack on the Twin Towers in Manhattan and the Pentagon in Washington, DC. Such unthinkable tragedies changed the entire nation. Everyone I know in New York suffered to some degree from post-traumatic stress disorder.*

At least I had an option out. I felt almost selfish and guilty for wanting to escape and leave others with no way out behind. Psychologists would have a name for that. I decided to have a wait-and-see attitude before making any decisions about leaving. That was more than a decade ago.

CHAPTER SIX
God Dispatches His Angels

"Call unto me, and I will answer thee, and show thee great and mighty things, which thou knowest not" (Jer. 33:3, KJV).

When I arrived in New York the summer of the year 2000, I had called David and Marian Lewis, former lead singer of the group Atlantic Starr and former Olay spokesperson and model, to let them know I was in New York. I had first met the couple on another visit to New York in 1998 when they came to the Linden Seventh-day Adventist Church to share their story. After that, they came to Jamaica in early 2000 to minister in concert. I went to see them then, and I told them that I was planning on being in New York that summer. Marian gave me her number and told me to call whenever I was in New York. I ended up babysitting for that lovely Christian couple and went with them on a road tour as they went from state to state around the country sharing their testimony of how God brought them *Out of the Darkness into His Marvelous Light.* That was the theme of the tour I embarked on with them in the late summer to early fall of 2000.

When we got back to New York, I found another babysitting job that allowed me to save some money so I could start my first semester at York College in January 2001. A dear friend, Jaqui, who attended the same church I went to in Jamaica and was now living in New York, provided me with room and board for a year and a half until I was able to find my own lodging.

I usually visit the United States annually, staying either in Florida or New York each time. I first traveled to this country when I was 14 years old

CHAPTER SIX God Dispatches His Angels

with my mom. I remember my brother had traveled first with our dad, and then I came with my mom. My mom and dad have always been traveling back and forth on a yearly basis for vacation. I started doing that also in my twenties, in addition to performing in Indiana, Illinois, and New York and never entertained the thought of living in the US. It was not until an incident that took place one night on the very pathway where I lived that totally shook me up and let me started having thoughts of migrating.

One night while at home in my bedroom, I heard gunshots firing. I heard the shots hitting the wall as our house was on a corner lot with the front on a pathway and the side and back facing an adjacent street. I was so frightened. There was gang warfare in the housing development from time to time, but none of it came this close to home. I ran to the living room and hid under a table that was situated against a wall, but my feet were hanging out.

"Dear Lord, please don't let me die, not tonight," I prayed.

I was shaking under the table and did not even think to curl my body so that my feet would not hang out in plain view. I saw someone run inside the house and into my brother's bedroom. I immediately thought that it was my brother's friend but wasn't sure which one it was. My brother was lying in his bed. My grandmother was in the living room, my mother was upstairs, and my stepfather was outside washing the car. The gunshots were ringing out loud and rapid. I could hear them hitting the wall outside upstairs and downstairs. I don't remember ever being so frightened.

After the sound of the gunfire died down, I crawled from under the table and ran into the arms of the person I thought was one of my brother's friends. Only to hear, "Nuh worry man, a me dem a fire after."

("Don't worry, I'm the one they're shooting at.")

What! I ran upstairs to my mother's room and told her. By the time I got back downstairs, he was gone. Thank God, the shooters didn't see him run in the house because the gate was left wide open. My brother said the guy running from the gunshots had jumped into his bed to hide. I was beyond shaken up. I could not believe what was happening. A day or two later, I was alone at home and heard more gunshots. This time a young lad was shot in front of the house next to mine, right on our pathway. He died. It turns out he was not involved. They were looking for his brother.

What if I was outside? I thought. I could have been out there watering the plants or talking to a neighbor. I was a bundle of nerves. I just didn't feel safe anymore. I asked God to help me move from the neighborhood. Overall, it was safe most of the times with a few isolated incidents here and there, but things seemed to be changing for the worst.

At night I prayed, "Lord, please let your angels walk up and down this pathway and please let the idle boys see them so they won't fire any more shots."

God hears. God cares. I started relaxing a little bit. I was not as nervous. I was able to go outside and visit my neighbors. One day, my cousin Ted said to me, "Last night, I was outside with my friend from up the road, you know him. We saw some soldiers walking on the pathway and none a dem a nuh six foot!"

(Last night I was outside with my friend from up the road, you know him. We saw some soldiers walking on the pathway; not one of them was six feet tall!)

I asked, "What do you mean?"

He said, "They were so tall! So tall that my friend said, "It look like dem send out all of the tall soldiers tonight. Dem nuh have to jump gully; dem can just step over!"

(It seems they've sent out all the tall soldiers tonight. They do not have to jump over gullies, they can simply step over!)

I said, "Ted, it sounds like oonu see angels!"

(Ted, it sounds like you guys saw angels!)

"No," he replied, "They were soldiers."

It was after I went inside and thought more about it that I realized God had answered my prayers and let Ted see the angels and tell me so that I could know He had answered. What a caring God! I was not going to hear it from the idle boys, so the Lord let Ted see them and tell me about it. I was so thankful that God actually dispatched His angels to walk on the bloody and tainted pathway at my request. I thanked him for hearing a frightened girl's prayers. I knew God answers prayers, but it made me realize how much He cares. He didn't have to send His angels, but He did in answer to my request. I felt humbled and grateful. That answer to prayer helped to solidify my faith that God hears and God cares.

A few months went by, and the area regained some sense of normalcy, but to this day when I hear a loud noise, I get frightened and think shots are being fired.

CHAPTER SEVEN
Right on Time

After God came through for me following that episode in the assistant dean's office, I decided I was going to show up for class even though I did not yet have the money for the new semester. I was happy that my outstanding balance was paid and decided to trust that God would finish what He started regarding my college education. I decided I had nothing to lose by showing up for classes. I couldn't think of anything else to do. So there I sat in French class hoping that the professor would not single me out when she did not find my name on the register. Towards the end of the class when the professor said she didn't have my name on the register, I told her that my Father didn't send the money for me to pay for my registration yet.

I told my journalism professor the same thing. I was trusting God. I was not sure if I explained the situation in detail if any of the professors would understand that I am simply attending college by faith. I just prayed that God would come through before it was too late for me to make a down payment on the current semester.

I told a college mate about my situation, and she said she had seen people get called out of class because they owed the college. I worried about this while I sat in class, but at the same time, I begged God to help me, so I did not have to quit the degree program. I qualified for scholarships because I was getting good grades but my status as an international student disqualified me from such scholarships. I also was not entitled to any financial aid as an international student. I secretly joked to myself about being America's stepchild. I was not entitled to the benefits the legitimate children enjoyed.

The rate of exchange between the Jamaican and the US dollar made it difficult for me to get money from home. The sliding Jamaican dollar was approximately $60 Jamaican to $1US at the time. All these factors made my situation rather difficult, but I knew that nothing was too hard for God.

I remember one day being at home and cleaning the bathtub when I just burst out crying to God with such a loud wail that I was almost sure the residents in the neighboring apartment heard me.

"I can't believe You're letting this happen to me!" I screamed at God. "I can't believe You've let it come to this. It's like You're leaving me out in the wilderness."

I just stayed bent over the tub crying, feeling alone and confused. The next morning I got dressed and headed for the campus. As I turned the first corner at the end of the block to walk to the school, I heard a voice say, "Just write them a check."

> *Common sense was telling me there is no money so I must be crazy, but faith was speaking and saying watch what God is going to do. I begged God to increase my faith because I knew it made no sense praying if I was going to continue worrying.*

Huh? I did not have any money in the bank. However, I knew if I could cover my outstanding balance of $1,000, my registration for the new semester would not be dropped. I headed straight to the bursar's office, wrote a check for $1,000 and started fretting and praying. Common sense was telling me there is no money so I must be crazy, but faith was speaking and saying watch what God is going to do. I begged God to increase my faith because I knew it made no sense praying if I was going to continue worrying.

In the evening my friend Heather from my church in Jamaica, who was now residing in Florida, called me to find out how I was doing, and I told her my dilemma. She reminded me how I used to help her with bus fare and lunch money while she was going to college in Jamaica. I still don't remember. She told me because of my kindness to her in the past, she was going to send me $500. My friend Mekana in Bermuda called me that same evening to say she was going to send me another $500. I had the money to cover the check. The check did not bounce. God came through right on time.

> *"And it shall come to pass, that before they call, I will answer; and while they are yet speaking, I will hear" (Isa. 65:24, KJV).*

CHAPTER EIGHT
God Intervenes

God cares for every one of us. We are His beloved children. He wants to manifest His love for us personally in our lives—from the smallest detail to the greatest challenge—He wants to prove Himself strong on our behalf. We just have to trust Him. It became easier for me to trust God wholeheartedly when I had no other alternative. However, God wants us to trust Him all the time and with everything—every decision, every need.

God's word says in 2 Chronicles 16:9, NKJV, "For the eyes of the Lord run to and fro throughout the whole earth, to show himself strong in the behalf of them whose heart is perfect toward him."

Sometimes we face trying circumstances, and we focus on our problems instead of focusing on God. It is easy to do so, but God wants us to put everything in His capable hands. He has a solution when we in our finite minds cannot unravel our difficult situations. He knows exactly how to work things out because of His divine and infinite wisdom. Sometimes we lose sleep trying to figure things out; we stay up all night worrying about matters that we can't handle ourselves while our heavenly Father is just waiting for us to cast all our cares upon Him because He cares so much for us. We just have to trust Him completely.

More than anything else, God cares about our salvation. He sent His Son to save us. He made provision for us to be able to be saved into His kingdom from even before we have any knowledge of Him or any desire to serve Him. He seeks us out; He protects us, sustains us, and loves us whether we acknowledge Him or not. It has been said that God has "more

CHAPTER EIGHT God Intervenes | 29

than a thousand ways to provide for us," and He also has more than a thousand ways to bring us close to His side in total surrender to Him. He desires that every one of us would live for Him and inherit eternal life.

The well-known Bible text states, "For God so loved the world, that He gave His only begotten Son, that whosoever believeth in Him should not perish, but have everlasting life" (John 3:16, KJV). He truly loves each of us as if no other person existed and He wants us to be aware of how much He loves us. When we become truly aware of His love for us, we are inspired to love Him in return.

God will step into our lives and reveal His will to us sometimes when we least expect it. Sometimes we have plans for our lives, but sometimes God has other plans for us. For example, long before I embarked on my journey through college in New York, I had become a recording artist. I had a record distribution deal with Heartbeat Records in Massachusetts. However, just before my album was released, God stepped in.

I had read a book by Jan Marcussen titled *National Sunday Law* and learned that the seventh day is the Sabbath. I had no prior knowledge of the seventh day being a day of rest. I used to say any day could be the Sabbath. It is strange how we can read the Bible and not understand. What is even stranger is that we don't even realize that we are sometimes overlooking a fact that may even be blatantly explained and staring us straight in the face so to speak. Now, Exodus 20: 8–11 plainly states that "the seventh day is the Sabbath of the Lord."

So how did I miss that even though I had read it so many times? How did I naively think any day could be the Sabbath? It just shows how much we need the Holy Spirit to bring the things of God to our conviction. Otherwise, we come up with our own vain interpretation or end up following tradition. Not that tradition in itself is bad, but if it conflicts with God's word then we are opposing God.

Marcussen in his book plainly explained the original Sabbath and how it was changed throughout the course of history. I decided to do further research from a neutral source. This was in 1993, and in those days we didn't have the Internet, so I went to the library and did my research in the Encyclopedia Britannica. I realized that secular history also records the attempt to change the true Sabbath from Saturday to Sunday. I felt like I had been fooled all my life. I decided to take my stand with God and was baptized and became a Seventh-day Adventist. But I didn't quite know how to make the announcement amidst radio, television, newspaper interviews, and performances that came with the release of my album. I just told myself that my next album would be a gospel CD so I continued performing at various concerts, including Reggae Sunsplash, and appeared on many radio and television slots for interviews, as well as several newspaper interviews in Jamaica. I also did radio interviews in the United States to promote the album, and performed at various poetry cafes and university campuses. *Conscious* spent several weeks in the Top Ten on the College Music Journal (CMJ) charts. Still, God began opening and closing certain doors.

Becoming a Christian just before the release of my debut album was totally unplanned and totally unforeseen. I had written these songs/poems and set them to Reggae music before I became a Christian, and I had prayed to the Lord of creation before writing each song, asking Him to help me in my writing. I remember the Lord revealing Himself to me in dreams around this time even though I have worshipped Him all my life. It's as if He was giving me confirmation that He is the one true God of all creation. I call His name JAH on the album because that's the name Reggae artists use in songs. That name of God is found in Psalm 68:4 (KJV).

The years went by, and I continued writing, doing poetry and writing workshops, and performing. Today I find myself writing more about Him and His marvelous works. Yes, I still care about the injustices that are the theme of the tracks on my debut CD, and God cares too. He does not like injustice, and that is why He is going to bring an end to all the evils in this world. I read or watch the news and I am inspired to write, but the greatest thing is the knowledge that all inequality will come to an end. This is our hope, and this hope is not in vain; so God as conqueror will always be the theme of my writings. Even though the problems of the world still exist, He will be victorious and bring an end to crime and oppression.

God cares. He cares about our challenges and all our endeavors. He says through the prophet Jeremiah, "For I know the thoughts that I think toward you, saith the LORD, thoughts of peace, and not of evil, to give you an expected end" (Jer. 29:11, KJV).

God has certainly taken me on an adventure. If you want to go on a wonderful adventure, just let God lead you. Give all your plans and dreams to Him; you won't be disappointed. He definitely has bigger and better plans for you, even more than you can imagine for yourself. I have learned this over the years. It was not an easy lesson to learn—to totally "let go and let God." It took lots of learning reinforcements that came through various challenges. It took learning not to worry about tomorrow, and this came with experience as I let Him take over the reins on my journey through life. God is calling you to do the same.

CHAPTER EIGHT God Intervenes

The story of my faith journey with God and how He provided for me through college continues. I'll tell you more in the next chapter. God is eternally merciful, all-powerful and faithful. We just need to trust Him!

> *"Trust in the L*ORD *with all thine heart; and lean not unto thine own understanding. In all thy ways acknowledge him, and he shall direct thy paths" (Prov. 3:5–6, KJV).*

CHAPTER NINE

God Works Through Friends and a Stranger

I found work on campus as a writing, French, Spanish, and English as a Second Language (ESL) tutor. This took care of my living expenses, but the tuition was up to God to provide. I was friends with two sisters, Raquel and Trudy, and their boyfriends, Ted and David. Raquel is now married to Ted, and Trudy is now married to David. I remember it was near the end of the semester, and once again I found myself in the same situation where I owed the school and needed to pay the balance. I would not be able to know what my final grades were if I didn't clear my outstanding balance, and I certainly would not be able to register for the new semester. I cried on the phone one night to the two sisters. I could tell those girls felt distressed about my situation.

Raquel said, "Karlene, the Lord said to tell you that you will have the money on Sabbath."

I tearfully replied, "Okay, tell Him thanks." I did not want to doubt. I chose to hang on to those words.

That Saturday night after the Sabbath ended, Raquel called. She said, "Karlene, Ted and I took up a collection for you at New Rochelle during services today, and Trudy and David did the same in Springfield Gardens."

I was so moved by the generosity of these four friends. I was deeply touched that they would go as far as plead with congregations on my behalf. I thought about the generosity of those who donated and the mercy

CHAPTER NINE God Works Through Friends and a Stranger

of God who impressed upon their hearts to do so. God had shown Himself faithful once again and provided. Just like other semesters before, I had enough money to settle the balance with the college. I thanked them and thanked God.

God has been leading me, and He has been faithful in how He has provided for me to finish my studies. He came through so many times during those college years while I had no money that I told Him that this degree is definitely for Him.

There are other semesters that I recall being in the same predicament of not having enough funds. There were two common themes throughout my college career; one, not having any money for tuition and two, God providing for the tuition. Sometimes the way God came through for me would cause me to tell Him, "I will never, ever worry about anything again."

I remember it was near the end of the semester, and once again I found myself in the same situation where I owed the school and needed to pay the balance. I would not be able to know what my final grades were if I didn't clear my outstanding balance, and I certainly would not be able to register for the new semester.

I would feel almost embarrassed when He came through, and I reflected on how worried I was. I learned that the key to not worrying is to focus on the Supreme Provider and Problem Solver, not on the situation.

Help From a Stranger

I remember during another holiday break when it was almost time for the new semester to start, that I wondered how I would afford the money to register for the new semester. I remember it was summer, but I had not found any work. There is a book by Dr. Kenneth Mulzac, *Praying With Power Moving Mountains*, that I read frequently; so frequently that the book was losing its binding, and the pages were falling apart. I treasured that book because the author's experience was similar to mine. I had heard him speak and he had remarked, "This book is for anyone who has ever been in a crisis." I had read it before beginning my faith journey with God through college, but I have read it so many times since, especially during my college years. Dr. Mulzac relates in his book how God came through for him so many times that it inspired me to trust God with my challenges. It made me remember that God loves a challenge, because it gives us the opportunity to see just what a mighty God He is.

Well, during the aforementioned holiday break, I thought of Dr. Mulzac and decided to call the number listed in the book to contact him to let him know how his book had influenced and inspired me.

The number listed at the back of the book was for Oakwood College where Dr. Mulzac had accepted a position to teach after his graduation. I dialed the number and asked for him. The person on the other end of the line, a male, said he was no longer working there but had gone to the Philippines to teach. I told him my situation, how Dr. Mulzac's book had inspired me and that I regretted not being able to reach him because my situation was so similar to his, and I was hoping to share it with him. Then he responded, "Let me transfer you to the chaplain's office."

Professor Jeffrey Brown answered instead, and I told him the same thing I had just related with the other person who transferred me to him. He offered to pray with me, and then he said, "You have no money for college, and you're in New York. I know someone in New York who can help you."

Really? I thought.

He gave me the phone number and said, call this person, and tell him I said to help you. I called the number and shared my story with Rudy Sterling, the New York contact. Next thing I heard was, "Okay, can you come to services this Sabbath? I can meet you there and give you the money."

Just like that! He had never met me before. I was almost moved to tears. I was so touched by his generosity and the fact that God is so merciful and capable of handling my situation. God does work through people. There is no need to worry at all when we trust God. We might not be able to see a way out of our predicament, but God has a way out. He knows everyone everywhere and knows how to put us in touch with each other. No man or woman is an island. We are all brothers and sisters with a common Father who loves us dearly.

I felt comfortable with the fact that I was going to meet Rudy in a public place during a worship service. That Sabbath afternoon, in what seemed like a fairy tale, but was in fact really happening, Rudy counted out enough money for me to pay my balance and register for the new semester. What a mighty God we serve! God is truly amazing! To think I had never met Rudy before or the person who answered the phone or Professor Brown. I know this was all made possible by God himself, and

CHAPTER NINE God Works Through Friends and a Stranger

I love Him even more for caring so much for me. Just the same way He cares for you too; I can assure you of that. We can be assured of His everlasting love.

> *"The Lord hath appeared of old unto me, saying,*
> *Yea, I have loved thee with an everlasting love:*
> *therefore with loving-kindness have I drawn thee"(Jer. 31:3, KJV).*

CHAPTER TEN
An Immediate Answer to Prayer

When I stood up to give my prayer request at a weekly Wednesday night prayer meeting, I was not expecting the answer to be given immediately. I always enjoy prayer meetings. I love the songs we sing, the opportunity to present prayer requests and pray with others and for others, and most of all I love the testimonies. I really enjoy hearing what God has done for others. On this particular Wednesday night at prayer meeting, after I requested prayer for God's help in paying my outstanding balance and to for help in paying for the new semester ahead, a lady approached me.

> *"How much do you owe?" She asked.*
> *"Two thousand dollars," I responded.*
> *"Okay, I'll give it to you," she said.*

"How much do you owe?" She asked.

"Two thousand dollars," I responded.

"Okay, I'll give it to you," she said. "I'll just have to split it. I promised another student that I was going to help her, so instead of giving her the full amount, I'll give you half of what you owe."

You can imagine gratitude springing up inside of me, can't you? I thanked her, and she said, "No problem, that's what I do. I help students in college with their tuition."

CHAPTER TEN An Immediate Answer to Prayer | 37

God certainly has "a thousand ways to provide of which we know nothing" (*The Desire of Ages,* p. 330).

I was able to come up with the rest through babysitting jobs.

I remember one day sitting in my journalism professor's office. He was my mentor, and we were discussing the classes that I needed to take for the coming semester. I told him I had registered for six classes.

Professor Glenn Lewis dropped his pen. He looked me straight in the eyes.

"What's the rush?" he asked.

"I take six classes every semester because I need to graduate early," I responded.

"Karlene, you're very young," he protested.

Not really, I thought to myself.

I told him that because of my financial circumstances, I take six classes every semester. Because whether I take four to fulfill the requirement of being a full time student or whether I take six, the tuition is the same. So I take six classes per semester for economic reasons.

"Over-achiever," he said jokingly and approved the registration for eighteen credits for the next semester.

In order not to experience an overload, I would take two easy classes like physical education and music in addition to the required four classes. This way, I didn't have six subjects that all required much studying. That was my way of getting all those classes in without experiencing a burnout.

I had declared a French major when I first started my BA program without even thinking about the day in my bedroom in Jamaica where I got a revelation that I would pursue English at a university. It had just come to me like an unconscious thought. I remember questioning in my mind, why would I pursue an English degree?

Well, God knows the end from the beginning. During the month of December, 2003, I was looking through the college bulletin to see which classes I needed to take for the new semester. I was pursuing journalism as a minor, which by going through the bulletin, I realized fulfilled the requirements toward the English major. It then dawned on me that I could graduate a semester early if I switched things around and became a French minor instead. I was so happy about this. Given my financial situation, I wanted to graduate as soon as possible.

It was not until I decided to declare English with an emphasis in journalism as my major and French as a minor, that I recalled the revelation that I would pursue English at a university. God is truly beyond remarkable. Taking an English major was not a plan of mine even when I started college. That day in my bedroom, I didn't yet know where I was going to attend college. At the time the revelation came to me, I was thinking perhaps it would be the University of the West Indies since I was living in Jamaica then. Still, I had questioned, why would I pursue English?

God sees and knows everything from the beginning of time to the end of time.

I rejoiced that I would graduate after just one more semester and be able to put these difficult days of financial deprivation behind me. I was tired of owing the school every semester.

After I registered for classes for my final semester January, 2004, someone from the bursar's office told me a scholarship was there for me.

What? After all these years! It was one of those "final semester, you've done well" scholarships. Was I excited? Of course, I was!

The scholarship covered a portion of the tuition and a friend, Juliett, with whom I prayed almost daily, who attended the same church with me in Jamaica and was also now living in New York, took out a personal loan so I could pay the balance, with the arrangement that I would reimburse her monthly.

I reflect on this journey, and I am truly grateful. I could not do it by myself. God, family, friends, and relatives all contributed to me receiving my degree in June, 2004. I graduated with honors and received the award for Distinguished Achievement in Journalism, all to the glory of God. I am so glad I persevered through the tough times; always reminding myself that God did not bring me this far to leave me now. I had to persevere. I always remembered how He led the children of Israel through the wilderness; how He did not leave them in the wilderness, but brought them safely to the Promised Land. God always finishes what He starts. As the psalmist wrote,

> Many, O LORD my God, are Your wonderful works
> Which You have done;
> And Your thoughts toward us
> Cannot be recounted to You in order;
> If I would declare and speak of them,
> They are more than can be numbered.

God made a way so that I could afford a $3,800 per semester college tuition even though I had no money to begin with when I went to register that day in August of 2000. For any Jamaican not earning US dollars, that is quite a feat. God is good. He took me on a three-and-a-half-year

CHAPTER TEN An Immediate Answer to Prayer

journey of learning to trust Him and prove Him that He is faithful to His promise to be there for us when we call upon Him. This experience with God has built my faith, as I got to prove Him over and over when my back was against the wall, and I had no alternative but to trust Him. He saw me through difficult circumstances and sometimes placed me in situations where despite my trying to figure a way out, despite my worrying, I could do nothing else but surrender and trust Him, and He has never failed me. He never disappointed me. I got to know Him better, and this journey with Him has definitely increased my faith. I know Him personally as El Shaddai, the Almighty God with whom nothing is impossible.

Don't be afraid to trust in the Lord. Shall not the Lord of creation deliver? Shall not the Lord of creation provide? Praise God for His mighty acts towards us.

"It is He that hath made us, and not we ourselves" (Ps. 100:3, KJV).

CHAPTER ELEVEN
He Leads Me

"He leadeth me beside the still water.
He restoreth my soul" (Ps. 23:2–3, KJV).

After graduation in 2004, Juliett, the same friend of mine who had taken out a personal loan for me, called to say Linden Seventh-day Adventist School was hiring teachers for the summer. I went in and was hired to teach grades four through eight. January of 2005, I was hired as a newspaper reporter for a local paper in Queens. I was also teaching English as a Second Language (ESL) classes to adults at a community center in the Bronx in the evenings.

While working at the newspaper, I met a seasoned reporter at a function. He was at the time working at a radio station in Manhattan. He became somewhat of a mentor to me and encouraged me to pursue a master's degree. I had this in mind, but I had decided that I wanted to do so after I had saved enough money. However, two years went by, and I still did not have any money saved up for the degree program.

I would often talk to God and tell Him that I want to pursue a master's degree, but the journey on the way to having a bachelor's degree was so rough that I did not want to repeat it.

"Yes, I've learned to trust You, but the journey was just too difficult," I told God on several occasions.

God is merciful, and He pays attention.

CHAPTER ELEVEN He Leads Me

One day my new journalism mentor said, "Having a master's degree will put you in a different category."

I told him the situation, and he encouraged me to try to get a loan, as having a student loan was not a bad debt situation to get in.

"There are good debts and bad debts," he said.

I decided to register and take out a school loan. However, a lawyer, Fred Rooney, who was at the time working at the City University of New York (CUNY) School of Law and whom I had met through work asked me how I planned to pay for the degree.

"I plan on taking out a loan," I said.

"Don't take out a loan," he responded. "I am not making any promises, but send me proof of your registration and the cost and let me see what can happen."

I remember that was a Friday afternoon and Monday he called to say, "Karlene, I got a grant for you."

I almost screamed and had to leave my desk because I was so excited.

"Where did this grant come from?" I asked him.

"A lady and her husband who help people going to public universities is going to help you," he replied.

I was so grateful. God was listening when I expressed to Him that the journey was really hard for me with my bachelor's. His mercy never fails. The grant I was receiving was going to cover my full tuition for the two-year program. God is so amazing!

Praise God from whom all blessings flow; Praise Him all creatures here below; Praise Him above, ye heavenly host: Praise Father, Son, and Holy Ghost!

While pursuing the master's program, I was hired for a job as a media relations officer in a hospital in Brooklyn. I then moved on to become deputy director of communications for a non-profit organization.

I graduated in May, 2008, with a Master of Arts degree in International Relations. Later that year in August, a recession hit the United States. I did not even realize what was happening when I lost my job. I thought for sure I would find another job in no time. I had received a redundancy package from my job that included paying me for the next two months as well as continuing my health benefits until then. I had an interview lined up for December, but the day before the interview when I had my clothes prepared and was looking forward to the prospect of working in a new position, I received a phone call from someone at the prospective company stating that they were canceling the interview because they were now on a "hiring freeze."

That term became a daily refrain on the news. Every day there were reports of people being laid off. Soon, there were reports of thousands of people filing for unemployment across the country. The phone calls for an interview were sparse and led to nothing.

I decided to do freelance writing and editing. Then next thing I realized several years had passed but no full-time employment. I questioned God.

"What are you doing, God? You have the power to influence someone to hire me."

I remember how He took me through my bachelor's program and how He provided for the master's program. I also realized that He was closing all doors. I felt like I was flogging a dead horse by continuing to seek employment.

One day a friend who lives in Canada told me her company was hiring, and that they had offices in some states in the US, including New York. I felt a ray of hope. As I looked at the company's website and browsed the career opportunities of this particular company, I realized there were no open positions in New York, and whatever positions that were available elsewhere were technical positions—way out of my field and scope of training. I felt hopeless. I was sitting in Queens Central Library on my laptop ready to apply to this prospective position I thought existed. I closed the laptop and left the library. As I walked outside, I decided to call 3ABN for prayer. I do this from time to time when I want someone to unite with me in petitioning the Throne. There were tears in my eyes as I told Mitch, who had answered my phone call about my situation.

"Have you ever thought of writing a book?" he asked.

"It's funny that you should ask me that. Why do you ask?" I responded.

I was taken aback because just the week before I had gone to the same library with my laptop and thought to myself, *I could write my book in a week if I sit here every day and just type the story God has given to me, this journey He has taken me on.*

> *I could write my book in a week if I sit here every day and just type the story God has given to me, this journey He has taken me on.*

I remember starting the first page but then decided now was not the time because it seemed like putting the story together would be harder than I thought. So of course when Mitch asked if I had ever thought of writing a book I was somewhat flabbergasted. I knew it was not coincidence, so I laughed as I told him that just last week I had sat down to do so. Mitch

CHAPTER ELEVEN He Leads Me | 43

prayed with me, and I decided I was going to focus and write this book. However, the bills were piling up, and I decided the most important thing was finding a job. Then I could write the book in my spare time. I thought to myself that it would take much longer that way, but I had no peace of mind with the overdue bills disturbing my thoughts. However, nothing was changing regarding my job search.

I remembered that before I lost my job I had expressed to someone that I don't feel like working in the secular industry anymore, and that I wanted to do ministry. I had set up an interview on 3ABN Radio for Danielle and Michael who had a local radio program, *Hear O Israel*. Danielle and Michael were Jews who had become Seventh-day Adventists, and they were working for the Lord in bringing other Jews and non-Jews to Christ. It felt good using my skills to help them get the interview, and I told Danielle that when I leave my current job I would like to go into some form of ministry.

Well, God reminded me that I had said those words, and then I realized that He was closing all doors. I developed a burning desire to do some form of missionary work or some other type of ministry. I truly did not want to return to secular work. This was always in the back of my mind but with the bills in the forefront, I seemingly forgot, or it just became something I felt I could not do right away because of lack of finances. However, God changed my way of thinking. He closed the doors so I could see straight. I began to feel like God was saying no to any opportunities in New York. Also, I have always dreaded winter. Being from a sunny island, I just cannot get used to the cold, dark, dreary, short days of winter.

"God, I will go anywhere you want me to go, please only make it somewhere warm because I don't like winter. God, I would really like to move to Florida," became my prayer in the spring of 2015.

Over the years spent in New York, every winter I have always felt like moving to Florida, and every winter I had prayed, "Lord, please give me the opportunity to move to Florida."

Well, it is said that no prayer is wasted, and this is true. The moment I decided to do whatever the Lord wants me to do, God started acting on my behalf to create new opportunities. The Holy Spirit brought me into a state of mind where I completely surrendered the care of my bills to God. He did this through many interviews I watched on 3ABN. I would see countless interviews of people who had an experience with God that were compelled to tell their story and do some manner of work for Him. I would think as I watch those interviews, *Lord, You have given me a story too. I know I am to do something, but I just don't know exactly what.*

One particular young lady's interview hit me over and over as she spoke. Her name was Melodious Echo Mason. Her concerns were so similar to mine in that she worried about the bills as she felt impressed to give up her full-time employment. The only difference was I had lost my full-time employment, but I had the same concern of fulfilling my financial obligations. Melody, as she is called, decided to follow God's leading, holding on to the promise found in Matthew 6:31–33 (KJV).

> Therefore take no thought, saying, What shall we eat? or, What shall we drink? or, Wherewithal shall we be clothed? (For after all these things do the Gentiles seek:) for your heavenly Father knoweth that ye have need of all these things. But seek ye first the kingdom of God, and his righteousness; and all these things shall be added unto you."

I said, "Lord, I know that's what I am supposed to do, 'take no thought,' so I am going to fully trust You and finish writing that book I should have finished long ago."

I promised God that although the bills were long overdue, I would just leave it to Him to take care of them, because He has been doing so anyhow even though the payments were often late.

I tell you, I became a different person when I took on this frame of mind. I was totally happy and at peace. I had a new vision for my life. I felt like a weight had been lifted off me. It was during the writing of this book when I decided to not seek employment in the secular world anymore and just let God lead that He gave me a career opportunity that I was not looking for. Are you ready to hear it? Turn with me to the next chapter.

CHAPTER TWELVE
Working for the Lord

I would really like to move to Florida, I thought as I sat at my computer in my New York apartment one Sunday afternoon in May of 2015. I Googled "map of Florida." Over the past few days I had been praying and telling God in our conversation that it would be nice if I could move to Florida but in the country area—further north in that state and outside of the city areas.

"I just don't want another winter to catch me here in New York," I said to my mom.

"Why don't you look into Gainesville? Gainesville is nice," she replied.

I searched "House for sale in Gainesville." Ocala came up in my search and, compared to New York, the prices were beyond reasonable. Now, I couldn't immediately buy a house, but that's what I searched. I had the thought of selling my apartment and just moving to Florida.

Perhaps, I could buy a house with the sale of the apartment, I thought. As I viewed the homes in Ocala, I liked what I was seeing. Over the next few days, Ocala kept coming up in my thoughts. I didn't even know anyone in Ocala at the time, but it was like I was being led there. Four days later, I was again looking at homes in Ocala. I decided to Google "Adventist schools." Two schools came up; one of them was Shiloh Seventh-day Adventist School. I had my two-year-old in my lap, and I said to him, "Joshua, how would you like to go to Shiloh SDA School?" I said, "Let me call the school to find out what life is like in Ocala."

The principal answered the phone. I told him I was living in New York and looking to move to Florida. I asked him, "What was life like in Ocala?"

"Oh life here is like living in the islands," he said. "You can plant your own food in your garden. It does get cold around December or January, but by the afternoon it warms up again."

I liked the sound of that. It sounded like exactly what I was looking for—island life in a first world country. I told him how much I wanted to escape the New York winters.

"What is the tuition like?" I asked.

When I heard it would be half the cost of what it would be in New York, I was even happier.

"And if you work here, you pay less," I thought I heard. Looking back, he might have said, "If you go here, you pay less," but I heard "If you work here …"

"Oh, you have jobs there?" I asked, getting even more excited.

"Oh, we're looking for a teacher," he replied.

"I taught at an SDA School here in New York for the summer after I graduated, and I have taught and tutored adults, so I have some teaching experience," I told him.

> *God certainly does more than we ask or imagine. He certainly does the unexpected at times. As I type this chapter, I am packing and getting ready to move in two days. By the time you read this, I will have started working as a grade school teacher at Shiloh School.*

Within three weeks of that phone call, I was hired to teach at that school. Isn't God amazing? I called to find out if Ocala was somewhere I would like to live and how much it would cost to send my toddler to school there, and I got hired. God certainly does more than we ask or imagine. He certainly does the unexpected at times. As I type this chapter, I am packing and getting ready to move in two days. By the time you read this, I will have started working as a grade school teacher at Shiloh School.

"Now unto him that is able to do exceeding abundantly more than we ask or think, according to the power that worketh in us, unto him be glory in the church by Christ Jesus throughout all ages, world without end. Amen"
(Eph. 3:20–21, KJV).

Postscript

On the day I was about to submit this manuscript, I saw a tall, slender man in a brown suit speaking with our current pastor, Curtis Crider. It had been announced a few weeks earlier that Pastor Crider was going to be transferred, so we would get a new pastor. I was at a distance away in the schoolyard at Shiloh so I could not make out the face of the man standing in the church yard speaking to Pastor Crider.

I had not seen Rudy Sterling in several years; not since about the time of our meeting when he assisted me with my tuition after that one phone call based on the recommendation of Professor Jeffrey Brown. However, I knew instantly it was him. We had kept in contact sporadically but have not spoken in years. I knew Rudy had gone to Andrews University after we had met, and that he and his family were now living in Central Florida where he was working as a chaplain. Some minutes after, I saw Pastor Crider and asked him if that gentleman was Rudolf Sterling from New York?

"That's the man; that's the new pastor," Pastor Crider smiled and replied.

I could not believe it!

"I know him!" I responded.

"Well, go say hello," Pastor Crider chimed.

So as God would have it, Rudy Sterling is now the pastor of Shiloh SDA Church at the school where I teach. He didn't know of the book I was writing, but I was happy to update him on it and how God was working in my life since the time he helped me, a complete stranger.

It is that Pastor Sterling who has written one of the reviews for the cover of this book. I met up back with him just in time.

Never forget, God is working in your life as much as He has been and still continues to work in mine. Just pay attention, and put your trust in Him.

Epilogue

God has been working in your life; I am sure of it. He is active in our affairs, but sometimes we call it coincidence or we just don't pay attention. Life is not a bed of roses for anyone at all because we live in a world with forces of good and evil, but if we align ourselves with God, He will order our steps, protect us, provide for us, and prove Himself to be our Sustainer, Provider, Redeemer, Eternal God, and Friend.

Whatever life has been like for you, I am sure at times as you reflect you know that it could not have been anybody but God. It is our experiences with Him that strengthen our relationship with Him. The trials become a blessing after we have been through them, and they serve to strengthen our character. Of course, nobody likes trials, but they will come. King David said, "Many are the afflictions of the righteous: but the Lord delivereth him out of them all" (Ps. 34:19, KJV).

God delivers us from our trying circumstances by comforting us, providing for us, sending help to us, and so much more according to what each situation requires if we stay focused on Him.

How do we respond when trials come? Do we draw closer to Him or do we forsake Him? In times of trials, we should trust Him even more, feasting upon His word to strengthen us during the tough times and holding on to His promises. Sometimes it is easier said than done but this is only if we choose to focus on our trying circumstances and not on the Master of the solution to every problem. If we recall His power—try recalling His mighty deeds in Scripture, what He has done in our lives, what He has done in the lives of others who speak of His merciful acts towards them—if we do this, we will find it not so difficult to focus on Him as the Almighty—the One with whom nothing is impossible.

Just think about how He spoke this world into being, this earth we walk on exists because He said, "Let dry land appear." Think about how He parted the Red Sea and how the mixed multitude crossed on dry land in the midst of the sea; He parted the Jordan River for them, too. Think about how He provided manna in the wilderness; how He let water flow from a rock in the desert; how He became one of us, how many miracles he worked as Son of Man; how He died for us so that we may live with Him eternally. Oh, how He loves us! Think about how He breathed life into you and me. God is willing and able to do what is thought to be impossible with man; just trust Him with your life. Won't you?

It has been said, "We have nothing to fear for the future, except as we shall forget the way the Lord has led us, and His teaching in our past history" (*Life Sketches, p. 196*).

> *"The LORD is my rock, and my fortress, and my deliverer; my God, my strength, in whom I will trust; my buckler, and the horn of my salvation, and my high tower"* (Ps. 18:2, KJV).

Bibliography

White, Ellen G. *The Desire of Ages.* Mountain View, CA: Pacific Press Publishing Association, 1898.

White, Ellen G. *Life Sketches of James White and Ellen G. White 1880.* Battle Creek, MI: Seventh-day Adventist Publishing Association, 1880.

We invite you to view the complete
selection of titles we publish at:
www.TEACHServices.com

We encourage you to write us
with your thoughts about this,
or any other book we publish at:
info@TEACHServices.com

TEACH Services' titles may be purchased in
bulk quantities for educational, fund-raising,
business, or promotional use.
bulksales@TEACHServices.com

Finally, if you are interested in seeing
your own book in print, please contact us at:
publishing@TEACHServices.com
We are happy to review your manuscript at no charge.

www.ingramcontent.com/pod-product-compliance
Lightning Source LLC
Chambersburg PA
CBHW042137160426
43200CB00019B/2962